The Way Of Wealth

The Way Of Wealth

*Principles of success for
your personal wealth journey*

Jason Fennimore, Evan Yaros
& Scott Alexander

XULON PRESS

Xulon Press
2301 Lucien Way #415
Maitland, FL 32751
407.339.4217
www.xulonpress.com

© 2021 by Jason Fennimore, Evan Yaros & Scott Alexander

All rights reserved solely by the author. The author guarantees all contents are original and do not infringe upon the legal rights of any other person or work. No part of this book may be reproduced in any form without the permission of the author. The views expressed in this book are not necessarily those of the publisher.

Due to the changing nature of the Internet, if there are any web addresses, links, or URLs included in this manuscript, these may have been altered and may no longer be accessible. The views and opinions shared in this book belong solely to the author and do not necessarily reflect those of the publisher. The publisher therefore disclaims responsibility for the views or opinions expressed within the work.

Scripture quotations taken from the King James Version (KJV) – public domain.
Scripture quotations taken from the Holy Bible, New Living Translation (NLT). Copyright ©1996, 2004, 2007 by Tyndale House Foundation. Used by permission of Tyndale House Publishers, Inc.
Scripture quotations taken from The Message (MSG). Copyright © 1993, 1994, 1995, 1996, 2000, 2001, 2002. Used by permission of NavPress Publishing Group. Used by permission. All rights reserved.

Printed in the United States of America

Paperback ISBN-13: 978-1-6628-3572-8
Hard Cover ISBN-13: 978-1-6628-3573-5
Ebook ISBN-13: 978-1-6628-3574-2

Table of Contents

Prelude vii

1. Maybe There is a Better Way? 1
2. Traditional Financial Concepts 5
3. Real Wealth Principles 14
4. Family Banking 19
5. Generational Planning 28
6. The Entrepreneur 32
7. God's Economy, The Blessing 42
8. Philanthropy & Giving 51
9. Get on Your Way of Wealth 58

Prelude

"Enter through the narrow gate..." Matthew 7:13

*"... the LORD God stationed mighty cherubim to the east of the Garden of Eden. And he placed a flaming sword that flashed back and forth to guard **the way** to the tree of life." Genesis 3:24*

According to one line of ancient jewish thought, it is said that these cherubim which guarded Eden possessed faces and bodies that resembled the gryphons of legend- creatures that were described as guarding stores of wealth, having the resemblance of both the lion and the eagle.

We pray that this book will begin to open your mind to the wealth of Eden that is still available to us today and the blessings ready to be returned to God's children. We believe that "the wealth of the wicked is laid up for the righteous," as Proverbs 13:22 says. and through following the principles taught in this book you will begin to receive the full harvest God has for you!

The Way of Wealth

"Then you shall see and be radiant; your heart shall thrill and exult, because the abundance of the sea shall be turned to you, the wealth of the nations shall come to you." Isaiah 60:5 (ESV)

We want the reader to know that this book is for everyone- even if you are not a follower of Jesus. We want you to know that no matter who you are or what you have done in your life, Jesus loves you beyond what any human description could express to you. He has always loved you, and has always pursued you. Yet there is a force of evil in this world that may have been fighting to keep you away from him- whispering in your ear about your past, creating doubt in your mind that God's desire for your life is always good by placing difficult circumstances in your way. We want you to experience the grand plan of your Heavenly Father through the area of finance in this book. Did you know that Jesus talked more about money than heaven or hell? That's because money is a vital piece of quality of life. It isn't really about the money, it's about the life that we were supposed to live, the life that He originally planned for us to live.

I urge you to decide today whom you will serve. Will you continue to give ground to the doubts and shadows that have been lurking about all of your life? Or will you surrender your life to your Creator? There is no longer any time to waste.

CHAPTER 1
MAYBE THERE IS A BETTER WAY?

"Let no debt remain outstanding, except the continuing debt to love one another, for whoever loves others has fulfilled the law." Romans 13:8

Why do we stick to the status quo, without ever thinking of the other possibilities that are out there to choose from? For most of our lives, we are told we can become anything we want–that we can do anything we can dream of! But this idea of becoming whatever we want, in reality, is the same for everyone. We are taught the same cycle of life: get good grades in school, get a college degree, take out large sums of debt, work for 40 years, and retire at 65 to enjoy retirement for 15 years. The system above works for some people, but most often people have jobs they do not enjoy or exhaust them and they live their lives for the weekend. What if there is something else out there? Something we can enjoy each day of the week and never desire to retire from?

The Way of Wealth

If you were asked if you wanted to be like everyone else, you would probably say no. We all want to be unique and stand out on our own. We want to become the person God created us to be, not who our parents, friends, and teachers tell us to be. The system around us encourages us to be a slave to our job and to debt. The system pushes debt, unhealthy eating habits, employment and superficial education.

There is a certain way we are programmed to live and think, but that is not the right way. For example, is taking out $30K in student loan debt to learn information you can find for free on the internet the best investment? Of course this depends on your career desire, but how many people do we know who have a degree that they never used? If you want to be an engineer, nurse, doctor, or several other careers, you need the degree, however, there are so many opportunities that require only hardwork and determination. The best investment is in yourself. Never stop learning and growing for yourself.

"Formal education will make you a living; self education will make you a fortune!"–Jim Rohn

Question Everything

What happened to learning about the basic skills? Writing a check, doing your taxes, how to get a loan, what is an interest rate, the list goes on and on. Education has been about passing tests rather than learning skills that we will actually use in our daily lives. How many people never learn practical life skills and it becomes a disadvantage?

Why are we working for someone else for our whole life, building their dreams and never our own? At some point in time we have to escape from the system. We need to build our own dreams. Imagine the life you could build for your family if you educated yourself and pursued your dreams. You not only have the ability to earn money, but time. Time to spend with your family. Time to pour into others. Time to be who God created you to be.

In school we are taught everything from math, to reading, to history, to science, and so on and so forth. But when you look at yourself, there are a couple things that you excel in. It is a good thing to be educated in all areas, but in terms of earning a living, it is the people who are better than 99% of all the other people in one area who end up being the best. The idea of 'making it by' in our careers is never going to get us to where we want to be. If you want to be an accountant, you need to be the best one out there. If you want to have your own plumbing business, you need to be the company that goes above and beyond and stands out above all others.

"...let God transform you..." Romans 12:2

If you are willing to let go of your old way of thinking, this book will generate a massive amount

The Way of Wealth

of wealth for you in every area of your life. However, the information contained in this book will not help you if you are not willing to change the way that you think and the way that you live. Remember: This is not just about you, but your families, friends, children, and their children.

"Then why do these people stay on their self-destructive path? Why do the people of Jerusalem refuse to turn back? They cling tightly to their lies and will not turn around." Jeremiah 8:5

Some people will be stubborn, and continue in their old ways, and some will choose the new Way (really the Old Way, that has been forgotten) that we will outline for you. "I set before you this day life and death… but choose life!" Deuteronomy 30:19

CHAPTER 2
TRADITIONAL FINANCIAL CONCEPTS

The 401(k) Scenario

The way in which we have been taught to become 'rich' has led the vast majority of people down paths of mediocrity or devastation.

Let me begin with what I was taught–Go to college and graduate so you can get a good job and once you have that glorious job you can contribute to a wonderful thing called a 401(k) and you can retire at age 65. Unfortunately, as most reading this can imagine, life isn't so cookie cutter. That job that sounded so great while you were in college might not be so great–it might not even be in the field you studied! Oh, and that 401(k), it's a great product, but mostly for the investment firm managing your money. While you may hopefully receive a good return on your money, the investment firm earns money from you regardless of how your 401(k) performs! Whether your 401(k) grows 20% or loses 20%, the investment firm gets their fee.

Here's a simple example of how a 401(k) works. The 401(k) is a tax code that allows you to set aside money in an account without paying any taxes now, however, it will be taxed when you take it out. You can invest that money in various stocks, bonds, mutual funds, index funds, etc.. Later down the road between age 59 ½ and 70 ½ you can begin taking money out for retirement. If you want to withdraw money before your 59 ½th birthday you'll have to pay income taxes on that money and an additional 10% penalty, and you definitely don't want to wait past age 70 ½ to start taking withdrawals, you'll have to pay income taxes and a bonus 10% penalty! Usually bonuses are a good thing, but not in this case.

Another option is the Roth (or Roth 401(k)). This option allows you to put money into a retirement account with post-tax money, so you don't have to pay taxes later in the future. Between the 401(k) and the Roth 401(k), I use a simple analogy: would you rather pay your taxes now when you know how much they will be, or wait 30-50 years down the road when you have no idea what they will be. With the massive debt we have as a nation, I can only imagine that taxes will have to go up in the future to pay off that debt. You will still have many of the same restrictions you have in the 401(k), but in layman's terms, you won't have to pay any more taxes to Uncle Sam in retirement.

Traditional Financial Concepts

These retirement accounts work by you putting aside money each month, letting it grow over time, and one day, some day, you can retire. I'll refer to this as the accumulation method. This method works on the notion you invest money over the many years of your career and your money will compound throughout those years and suddenly you'll have enough to retire. The accumulation method is what's taught to us from family, friends, and maybe school, but it's not the only method available. Later I will show you the method used by the wealthy to build wealth at a much faster rate.

Let me tell you an example why I'm not a huge fan of the accumulation method in the 401(k) so you can better understand why I'm writing you these things. Someone I know was a casualty of the 2008 stock market crisis. He had a 401(k) at the company he worked for and it was invested in that company's stock. Not only did he lose his job that year, his company went out of business and that left his 401(k) worthless. Most people weren't invested in one stock like he was, but they still lost around 50% of the value in their 401(k) regardless. Now imagine this scenario: You lost your job, you don't have much money saved in your emergency fund and you need to withdraw $10,000 from your 401(k) to pay the bills. That $10,000 in your 401(k) was just worth around $20,000 before it dropped 50%, but not only that, you have to pay income taxes and a 10% penalty on that $10,000. What was once $20,000 in your 401(k) crashed to $10,000, and all the way down to something around $7,000 depending on your tax bracket plus the 10% penalty.

I know that sounds very doom and gloom, but that was the case for many Americans, including my friend (but worse). Like I said previously, life isn't so cookie cutter, and it becomes our personal responsibility to protect our financial house against the ups and downs of the stock market and the loss of a job. I can't protect you from losing your job, but I will show you later on how to protect yourself from the pitfalls of the 401(k).

Ultimately, our financial future isn't something to be left up to chance. Many people put money into stocks and mutual funds and have no understanding of the businesses they are buying into and how their investment will perform. Your financial future shouldn't be like throwing your money down at the casino, but most people do just that. They throw their money into some stock and just hope that it goes to the moon! There's a reason why the bank will lend people money to buy an asset (home, investment property, etc.), but not stocks.

Save For The Long Run

Unfortunately most people don't plan for their financial future enough, which leaves them in a rough spot later in life. Luckily, no matter your age, you can take the first steps toward saving and building wealth for your future. Start by writing down all the money you make and where it goes. If someone were to tell you 100 hundred different locations of buried gold in your city would you not pull out a pen and paper and write it down? You would probably ask for the exact coordinates to be sure you could find every last bit of the gold! That's exactly what you need to do to be successful in your personal finances so you can build wealth for yourself and your family.

I want to tell you the most important thing in regards to saving for your future–You owe it to yourself and your family to save and build wealth. Pay yourself first! Don't let the first bit of money you earn go to your mortgage, your car payment, your phone bill, or anyone other than yourself. It may be hard. It may be something you've never thought about, but do yourself and your family a favor and do it. Start with however much you can, but try to deposit the first 10% of your income into the Bank of You!

Educate Yourself On Debt–Home Ownership

There are many different types of debt and most people put them all in that one category: Debt. However, not every debt is even truly debt. One of the biggest 'debts' most people have in their lifetime is a mortgage, but used properly it can be the easiest way to become wealthy in your lifetime. It's estimated that 90% of millionaires did so through real estate! Maybe they didn't do so by just buying one home for their family. Maybe they purchased numerous properties. Regardless of that, the very thing they may have done at a larger scale than

The Way of Wealth

the average family can be done at a smaller scale to build wealth for you and your family. Let's do a minor calculation of home ownership vs. renting.

Let's say you purchased a $200k house with a 3.5% down payment loan ($7k down payment and loan of $193k) at a 3.5% loan, pay PMI, home insurance, and property taxes. Your payment each month will be around $1400. Home values average an increase in value of 3-5% each year, but for this illustration we will go with the more conservative of those–3%. Here is an easy table showing how much you'll pay each month,

Home Ownership	Year 1	Year 5	Year 10	Year 20	Year 30
Monthly Payment	$1400	$1400	$1235	$1235	$1235
Home Value	$200k	$225k	$261k	$350k	$471k
Loan Value	$193k	$173k	$144k	$88k	$0

*These numbers are rough estimates. Actual cost, rates, and figures will vary. PMI ends after 94 months.

Likewise, what would it look like if you decided to rent a home or an apartment instead–never purchasing a home? Unlike purchasing a home and having a mortgage, your rent will likely rise each year. I'll assume an increase of 2% each year to your monthly rent, which is slightly below the national average. We will also assume that everything, all included, will cost you even less than the cost of owning your own home–only $1300 per month to rent!

Renting	Year 1	Year 5	Year 10	Year 20	Year 30
Monthly Payment	$1300	$1407	$1554	$1894	$2309

*Assumes an average rent increase of 2%. Numbers rounded to nearest whole value.

Traditional Financial Concepts

I hope you're beginning to see the difference between these two options and the true cost of renting. I know someone might be thinking, "well, the person who rented never had to put $7k down as a down payment or spend money on keeping up the home." I hear you! But even so, assuming you invested that $7k into the stock market and averaged 8% every single year, you would be lagging behind at $109k after 30 years and still paying rent each and every month! The cost of upkeep on your home is also a minor cost in comparison to the $632k paid into rent those 30 years!

After 30 Years	Total Cost	Total Value	Monthly Payment
Home Ownership	$459k	$471k	$0**
Renting	$633k	$0	$2309

*These numbers are rough estimates. Actual cost, rates, and figures will vary.
**Will still have to spend money yearly on home insurance and property taxes.

This is meant to encourage you! Even if you feel like you're way behind and should have purchased a home years ago, you still can take the first steps towards learning about home ownership and how to get started. If you're still young and have the ability to invest in a home, take the time to do your research and learn the housing market in your area and don't be afraid to talk to several realtors in your area for advice and go with the best one for you and your family.

The Way of Wealth

Educate Yourself On Debt–Other Debt

What other types of debt are there? The most popular out there are car loans, credit card loans, student loans, and personal loans. These types of debts are much different than a mortgage and let's go over why that is the case. When looking at a debt you have to look at the equity, or simply put, the value of the item in which you have a loan/debt on.

A car loan is much like a mortgage in the sense you have collateral on your loan–the value of the car. However, as many people already know, the value of a car depreciates over time. This often leaves you with a car with a value much lower than the amount of money you put into it after paying off the loan. On average, a new car loses 60% of it's value after 5 years. Doesn't sound like the best investment!

Credit card debt is often the most snaring of them all, especially to younger individuals who haven't learned the true cost of not paying off those cards right away. Unfortunately, there's often no collateral on this type of debt (like the value of a car or a home). With an average credit card interest rate of 18%+, often even higher for those new to the credit card market, the amount you owe on your credit card can increase very quickly. With an interest rate that high your debt on your card, without any payment, can double in as little as 4 years! This can lead to a position that can be hard to escape and greatly lowers your credit score, leading to a much lower chance of qualifying for a mortgage later.

Getting an education can greatly increase your income potential after college, but it also can lead to a high student loan after those 4 years. The 'collateral' on a student loan is the information, knowledge, and degree you earned. If possible, before amassing a large student loan, know and understand what you enjoy doing and in which areas you are naturally gifted, so you have that much higher chance of success after completion. Just like any investment, know the ins and outs of your loan and how much it will cost after you graduate and how much you can expect to make in your career.

Many people have personal loans from banks, credit unions, online lenders, or from someone you know. They have terms and conditions and the rates can vary. These can be used in a good way, but for the average person, they get into loan debt because of an emergency and then they have to find a way to pay it off.

Some people do not like to look at their debt because of the power it has over them. The best thing anyone can do is seek help on their finances and get a plan on how to conquer their debt. It is one of those things that people do not like to talk about, but getting help as early as possible is the best thing to do. Have a plan and keep it!

CHAPTER 3
REAL WEALTH PRINCIPLES

The Reality of Real Estate

"Buy land, they aren't making any more of it."
–Mark Twain

There's an important lesson to be learned in that quote, and many never truly grasp it. There will never be more land than there is right now. No one is making more of it! Those who realize this fact can benefit from it greatly. They can purchase land, homes, commercial properties, and the value of those assets will always exist. The reason why I say that is because not everything we categorize as an asset is backed by anything physical.

There was once a time when the US Dollar was backed by physical gold reserves–they couldn't just print more bills without having more gold reserves. However, that changed in 1971, and to this day, the money we have is "fiat" money–it's paper with a promise from the government. Some might say, "well, it can still buy me stuff and it works for me," but if I asked that same person if they trusted the government with their money they might say otherwise. Owning physical wealth is much more important than owning printed money. At the end of the day, would you rather have a warm and inviting home, a family by your side, and food on your table or paper money, friends online, and takeout food? I know those aren't the best comparisons, but the idea stands true; real, physical things are of much more value than those that aren't.

The reason this is important is because people created the system of money and investing that we are taught about in school. God didn't create fiat money, He created real, physical things. There's something powerful about possessing gold, silver, land, property, and businesses. Owning real assets creates a true sense of ownership and you become the one in charge, not the people on the other side of the stock market who know how to take advantage of it. There should come a time in everyone's life where the reason they are successful financially isn't because of some luck that the market went up, but because they learned and took hold of their finances–they invested in themselves, not someone else.

Passive Income

Another great benefit of owning properties and businesses is the potential for passive income. The

The Way of Wealth

most important thing I can teach you from reading this book is to invest in earning money passively. The most common way people are taught to invest is for the long haul. Putting money away and letting it grow until you have enough to provide for yourself in retirement. There's nothing wrong with that. Many people can live a happy life doing that, but what about another option? What about passive income?

The thing with passive income that has all other options beat is that you can become financially free at a much earlier time and your income grows with time. What if you could invest in 3-5 investment properties that provide you with an additional $500 per month each? That would be an extra $1500 to $2500 per month straight into your pocket. Or maybe you invest in a small business and that provides you with an extra $4000 each month? Those are just easy examples in which you can have passive income.

The goal however is this: to create enough passive income to pay for all your expenses. If you can create an extra $5000 per month of passive income from any combination of investments and that $5000 pays for all of your expenses, you can officially retire whenever you like. You can work because you want to, not because you have to. You can give without worrying about paying a bill. You get to live a life free of the stress of worrying about money, and I think everyone could benefit greatly from doing just that.

Once you get a taste of the benefit of having money come to you passively, you will begin to understand the power of it. Additionally, with each increase in your passive income, the more money you will have to invest in assets. At first you may only have $100 each month of passive income, but as you continue to save that $100 each month and invest it into more assets that create passive income you will be able to continue to grow that $100 into a much larger amount. Set a goal for yourself, and your future self, as to how much passive income you want to achieve and when you want to achieve it–then start and never stop.

Real Assets Vs. The Silent Tax

There is a tax that many people never consider when they make and save money. Oftentimes we do not even think about it when we look into the past, but it is stealing your savings. The silent tax is inflation. Each year the value of the dollar decreases. Back in the 1970s the average home cost was around $24,000 and the cost of gasoline was 36 cents. How does that happen?

As I said before, the money we use is fiat money. It's just paper. And with paper, you can simply keep printing it and each year they continue to print money, the value of the existing money decreases. If you save your money and never convert it to real assets, the value will continue to decrease. Sometimes we see very wealthy people and we assume they must have tons and tons of money

The Way of Wealth

sitting in their bank account, but it's often the opposite. When the wealthy acquire money, they invest it. They turn paper money into real assets. We can do the same!

In order to beat inflation and grow wealth we need to make that switch. You are allowed to have some money in the bank, but don't leave it there to die. When you can, buy precious metals, land, properties, etc.. When you do that, your wealth will begin to grow. It is a very easy thing to do, but it does require learning and educating yourself on each form of asset you want to invest in. If you want to buy precious metals, learn the market and find trusted sources. Land? Find areas that have growth potential, learn about the tax advantages available, and become an expert in that field. Those are just a couple assets to consider, but the main thing each person needs to do is learn. Become an Investor, not a victim of the system.

MINDSET OF THE WEALTHY

Wealthy People			Average People
Invest in family bank	Invest in Real Estate	Invest in Business	Spend nearly everything
↓	↓	↓	↓
Spend on a new car	Spend on a dream house	Spend on vacations	Stay just over broke

CHAPTER 4
FAMILY BANKING

I want to ask a very simple question, not that it's a question you've heard often, but rather one that has a very easy answer. If a new bank location opened up near you and they offered an average rate of return between 4-6% guaranteed each year would you be interested? "Yes, why wouldn't I"? But if you are like me you would definitely have some serious questions. 'Is this a legitimate bank? Has this thing been around for more than a week? Seems sketchy.'

It was something I once thought, if I'm being honest with you. My number one go-to is skepticism when things seem too good to be true. But with some thorough research, it ended up being 'legit.'

The real reason for never hearing about this 'bank' is because it was hidden behind something that's gathered a bad reputation over time. The 'banking' method I learned about involves Whole Life Insurance–specifically overfunded, whole life insurance. It has been used for well over a 100 years by some of the most wealthy individuals and families to accumulate wealth and protect against loss. But with any great product out on the market, there's someone selling it, and unfortunately for the average whole life insurance consumer, the money made from selling whole life insurance isn't in selling overfunded whole insurance like the wealthy use, but rather underfunded policies that are full of fees and expenses. Something that the wealthy use to store and accumulate wealth was tainted by bad salesmen and saleswomen who were more interested in their own success rather than their client's.

There is still hope for the average person. The reason for this coming chapter is to explain how a family banking policy can be used to store and accumulate wealth and how to ensure you have a policy that is built specifically for you.

Family Banking Explained

There are a few key features which make a family bank so appealing:
1. You accumulate cash value in your policy you can utilize when you want.
2. There is a guaranteed interest rate–most often of 4%.
3. In addition to the 4% guaranteed, there are dividends which can add on average an additional 1-2% growth each year.
4. Whole life policies come with a death benefit which can provide your family with

financial support in your passing, and since it's whole life insurance your family will benefit from it whether you pass away at 30, 60, or even 100 years old. Leaving generational wealth to your family.
5. You can use your cash value in your policy to invest in whatever you choose (real estate, college, downpayment, vehicle, etc.)
6. The payments are flexible and you can contribute the max amount per year, or if times are tough you can contribute the minimum– each depends on your financial situation.
7. Payments into a whole life policy are after-tax dollars, and if structured correctly, all the growth in your policy is tax free.

There are many ways to use your family bank. You can start a business, pay off high interest credit cards, buy a vehicle, put a downpayment on a home, pay for a child's college loans, or whatever else you may have in mind. The beauty of it is that you get to decide. Instead of going to a bank to ask for a loan for a business you wish to start, you can borrow money from your cash value in your family bank to pay for it, and you can decide if you want to put the money back into your policy or not.

If you're reading this book and want an example of how this works, here are a few:
1. You've accumulated $50,000 in your policy and you are interested in replacing your car that's been having transmission issues

The Way of Wealth

for several months now. Instead of going to a bank and getting a loan for the next 60 months at an interest rate of 4%, you borrow $20,000 from your policy to pay for a new car in cash. Instead of paying the bank the interest for the next 60 months, you use the monthly cashflow you saved from not getting a car loan to pay back into your policy–allowing you to be your own bank!

2. You have been dreaming about starting your own business and you've always been very handy and a great craftsman. You realize there is a demand in the market for custom made wood picture frames online. You need money to buy the equipment, materials, and some extra money for marketing and you calculate that it will cost you $8,000 to get started. You've been building up your cash value in your family bank for several years and have $15,000 accumulated thus far. You sketch up some designs and buy a few materials to make up a demo and start a website. With everything in place you borrow money from your family bank to buy all that you need to start selling online and build the business you've always dreamt of starting! You never had to ask a bank or a family member for a loan, and you can pay yourself back on your own time.

Family Banking

3. Recently you noticed a for sale sign on a property you drive by on the way to work. You've always admired the rustic look this property had and never really thought about getting the chance to buy it. You come to learn that the owner has passed away and that the owner's children are selling the property because they all have homes of their own in another state. They have already received 2 offers just below their asking price of $160,000 but each of those are bank financed and they are in a hurry to sell. You have been building up the cash value in your policy for years and now have $180,000 in your family bank. Even though they have received an offer for $150,000 and for $152,000 from the other two buyers, you are able to offer something the other two couldn't–cash. You borrow $150,000 from your family bank and offer them $135,000 and are able to close the deal in a matter of days. You know you got a great deal based upon similar homes in the area, but your new property needs some work. After adding another $15,000 worth of work to the property it's now worth $200,000. Since you were able to buy the house at a great discount and only had to put $15,000 into fixing it up, your total investment was only $150,000. You decide to list the property for sale and get an offer for $200,000 and just profited $50,000 (minus closing costs

The Way of Wealth

and other costs). With the extra money in the bank, you pay back the full $150,000 into your family bank and have an extra $40,000+ to invest or save for the future.

4. When you got married 20 years ago you started your family bank with your spouse. Diligently you've both worked hard and have used your family bank to buy vehicles in the past as well as pay off your credit cards, but now your daughter is on her way to college. She enrolls and gets several scholarships, but after 4 years she finally graduates college. Unfortunately she still had to take on student loans of $18,000 for her classes that weren't covered by the money from her scholarships. You and your spouse decide to borrow from your family bank to pay off her student loans and set up an agreement with your daughter to pay you back $300 a month for 5 years without any interest once she finds a job. After a few months she is able to find a good paying job and can finally start paying you back. Since you borrowed from your family bank you were able to save her from having to pay the interest on a student loan along with giving her the peace of mind of not having her loan balance grow.

Those were just a few scenarios of how you can use a family bank to provide a benefit for yourself and your family. Each person and family have a unique goal for their financial future, and thankfully a family banking policy allows you to decide what you want to do with it.

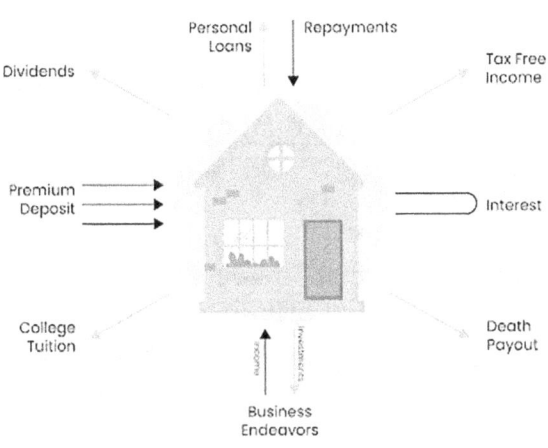

How To Know If a Whole Life Policy is Built Right

One of the first things I mentioned in this chapter is that whole life insurance has gotten a bad reputation over the years because many insurance agents who sell whole life policies were more interested in their commission than setting their clients up for success. Don't get me wrong, there is a place for minimally funded whole life insurance, but that's not why we use it. We use it because of the 7 features I listed before. Some whole life insurance agents may not even know how to use a whole life policy for family banking. They may have only been taught to use it one way, but luckily for you, now you know.

When searching for a whole life agent to set you up with your own family banking policy make sure they understand the concepts from before. If you're the one teaching them how it works, move on–quickly! Like I stated before, each person and family have different financial goals, so having a policy that is properly structured to meet your financial goals is key.

Look for options such as Paid-Up Additions and One-Year Term Riders. These features allow you to accelerate the amount of cash you are able to place into your family banking policy, while limiting the costs and fees. Doing that will allow you to accumulate cash value in your policy much faster and get to the break-even sooner and allow you to become your own bank.

In addition to those features, look for a whole life insurance company that has been around for a long time. Much like that analogy at the start of this chapter about asking how long this mystery bank has been around, you also want a life insurance company that has a strong financial history and takes care of its policyholders. One main thing to look for in taking care of its policyholders is to look for a mutual whole life insurance company. These companies will pay back to its shareholders (you, the policyholder) a dividend each year.

Getting Started On Your Family Bank

You do not have to be wealthy to start your family bank. You can start with what you can afford now and structure it for future growth. Each person has their own personal goals and each requires a plan custom to them. Whether you want to start your family bank to build wealth, invest, or have the security and peace of mind, you can do just that.

Imagine being able to open your own private branch of Wells Fargo for you and your family! Allow your wealth to grow and take advantage of investment opportunities whenever they come. Having guarantees on your money allows you to not worry about the small things, and instead, focus on the big picture and where you want to go.

CHAPTER 5
GENERATIONAL PLANNING

Planning to fund your family and future family is not always looked at in current times, however the earlier you realize this the better it is for everyone. Though you may think it's too late, it most certainly is not. You will need to look at what investment vehicles you currently have to know what actually will be passed down or depleted. For those who do not have any vehicles it is time for you to research and find the one that will benefit your family now and for later. It's hard to think that you can create generational wealth that goes beyond your sons and daughters, but the idea is simple once you are financially educated. Using the concepts we provided for you earlier in this book I urge you to look more in depth of those concepts and find the one that best fits you.

Wealth is not earned overnight, it takes time and energy to create wealth that will last generations. Educating yourself is extremely important to know what you can do to begin. This falls back onto the education system to ensure our youth are properly taught real financial concepts. A lot of concepts come from the bible and God laid them all out for you, now you must learn them and institute them into your life. Your parents or grandparents might have just saved money and put it into a bank or even kept it under that mattress or attic. The bad thing about that is that fiat currency (our US dollars) inflate and the value of that money decreases in time. That one dollar bill that your grandma had under her mattress could have the purchasing power of only .50 now. Holding onto large portions of money is not ideal nor does it help you against inflation.

Generational wealth is not just about having money, but knowing where your family came from and what your name means. Evan in Gaelic means "young warrior" and my last name Yaros originally Jaros comes from Czech and Slovak meaning "lively." My name means young lively warrior! I didn't realize how accurate this was until my good friend told me to look up the meaning of your name. God knows who you will be or become, which is amazing that a name you are given at birth can have so much meaning almost 30 years later! When it is time for you to have a family think hard about what you will name your children. They will become who they are named if they understand what their name means.

Proverbs 13:22 says "A good man leaves an inheritance to his children's children, but the sinner's wealth is laid up for the righteous." If this

The Way of Wealth

does not speak for itself then I am not sure what I can say that will change your mind. Earning your money morally right and fair will mean so much more than money earned by doing evil or being greedy. Money earned from evil or greedy ways will not be happily passed down. In Exodus 20:5 it talks about how sins are naturally passed down to the offspring. This is because children usually copy the parents as they were raised by them. You usually become who you are based on how you are raised and the environment you are in. By realizing this you must break free from these curses so you have a fruitful life full of abundance and success! How can you combat something that you are not intentionally responsible for? You must ask God for repentance, faith in the Lord and give your life to the Lord for then you will be free from generational curses.

We have all been to our grandparents' home many times and have had many family events there. But do you realize how hard they worked for that asset? Most likely no, our grandparents worked extremely hard so that they could afford to purchase that home and land. So that they could raise a family there and to make memories that last a lifetime. The question is why would you want to sell that? Your grandparents worked hard for that and now that they have passed you are going to sell it for profit or to purchase your own home? But they already gave you an asset, their home. They passed that asset to you as generational planning. They knew that one day it'll be you who would

Generational Planning

take that asset and for you to use it for your family. Hold on to as many assets as you can and manage them wisely. More responsibility is a good thing not a bad thing.

It is our hope that from reading this that you learned something new and that you will take the first step toward generational planning. It might not be easy at first for some and it might come second nature to others, regardless it is the first step to generational wealth! I charge you to see what your name(s) mean and to see how they reflect your current life or what potential you have. Think about that home your parents own or the home you currently have. Do they or you know what to do next with it?

"Wealth gained hastily will dwindle, but whoever gathers little by little will increase it." Proverbs 13:11

Chapter 6
The Entrepreneur

"Again, the Kingdom of Heaven can be illustrated by the story of a man going on a long trip. He called together his servants and entrusted his money to them while he was gone. He gave five bags of silver to one, two bags of silver to another, and one bag of silver to the last—dividing it in proportion to their abilities. He then left on his trip.... After a long time their master returned from his trip and called them to give an account of how they had used his money."
—Matthew 25:14-15, 19

The word for entrepreneur in hebrew is "yazam" which also means "initiator." An entrepreneur is a person who INITIATES ACTION.

What do God and entrepreneurs have in common? There are many things God and entrepreneurs have in common, but we will only cover several in this book:

Vision

Vision is one of the essential ingredients in the formula for being a successful entrepreneur. It is also a vital piece of who God is! Vision is seeing the end from the beginning. It is natural for us as human beings to begin by planning from beginning to end- but that isn't how God does it. He "begins with the end in mind." An entrepreneur is a person with God-sized dreams, but one whose God-sized dreams have God-type of plans. I'm sure you know the phrase "the devil is in the details." But even more so, GOD is in the details! Just try to read the books of Numbers and Leviticus in the Bible. Let's just say that they aren't the most engaging books out there. However, just because they are the least interesting doesn't mean that they are the least important. God almighty laid out these books in specific detail for us so that we would have exactly what we needed to live this life to its fullest extent.

An entrepreneur must be just as specific in the way that he/she goes about designing their company based upon their vision. Another word for vision is foresight, which refers to the idea of SEEING before it becomes reality. Biblically speaking, prophets were also referred to as "SEERs"- someone who sees something through supernatural insight that will come about in the future in another reality before it appears in this reality. An entrepreneur possesses a special gift of sight that defies limitations and believes for more than the natural eye can see!

The Way of Wealth

Proverbs 29:18 says, "Where there is no vision, the people perish…" Vision is a necessity for abundant life. An entrepreneur has vision!

Creation

I'm sure that at some point in your life you have heard some variation of Genesis 1:1…"In the beginning God created…" Here we see that God is a creator! I guess it would be more accurate to say that He is THE Creator. He created the planets, the earth, animals, and plants, but the one thing He created that is different from the rest of creation is mankind. We stand out because God chose to make us in the image and likeness of Himself! "So God created human beings in his own image." (Genesis 1:27) Now, this was in the very beginning, when all was perfect and right. Man ultimately decided against God's plan and opted to take sides with Satan and make his own plans. The consequence of this was that man could no longer partake in the plan of God- until God made a way to bring mankind back to Him through the sacrifice of Himself in the form of Jesus. Now, through Jesus, any person can become a part of God's family. It doesn't matter what your background is, it only matters if you'll accept God's free gift. If you are a part of God's family, God says that you are "In Christ." Colossians 1:15-16 says, "Christ is the visible image of the invisible God. He existed before anything was created and is supreme over all creation, for through him God created everything in the heavenly realms and on earth. He made the things we can see and the things we can't see—such as thrones, kingdoms, rulers, and authorities in the unseen world. Everything was created through him and for him."

Romans 8:17 says that "...since we are his children, we are his heirs. In fact, together with Christ we are heirs of God's glory." As God's children, we are heirs of the same things that Jesus is heir to. One of the attributes of Jesus is that "all things were created through him.." (Colossians 1:16) So, if we are heirs with Christ, we also then are able to let God create through us. This is the basis of creation for the entrepreneur, whether he gives God glory for his ability to create or not.

There are three steps in the creation of a thing: Thinking, Speaking, and Acting. The first step in the process of creation is to THINK about it! One must hold the image of what they want to create in their mind. This image must be clear and definite in its construction. The second step in the creation of a thing is to SPEAK about the thing that you have designed within your thinking. "Death and life are in the power of the tongue." (Proverbs 18:21) Have you ever noticed that it was WORDS that God used to create everything? The Bible says that God spoke, and then there was light! (Genesis 1:3) The last step in the creation process is the acting step. In Genesis 1:26, God speaks about creating humankind, but in Genesis 2:7, we see that God puts physical action behind His words of creation. God created man from a combination of the dust of the ground, and His very own breath! So, we have the three steps of creation.

If man is to create anything at all, he is to follow these three steps.

Spirit of Leadership

Throughout the Bible, there is one animal that God continually likens himself to, the lion! Hosea 13:7 says, "I will be like a lion unto them..," and Proverbs 30:30 describes a lion as.. "...mighty among beasts, who retreats before nothing.." Have you ever wondered why the lion is referred to as the "KING OF THE JUNGLE" when he is not the biggest, strongest, smartest, or fastest animal? It is because of the attitude that he carries. As the verse says, he "..retreats before nothing.." The lion has the "spirit of leadership." This is the same "spirit" that the best entrepreneurs operate in as well. They hunt down their "prey," (or sale, in terms of business) retreat before no obstacle, and are masters at leading their "pride" or "team" of people. So, if you want to be like God, and want to be the best entrepreneur possible, study the lion. Study his mindset, habits, attitude, and actions.

It is also worth noting that lions typically travel in their prides with numbers that can reach 30-40, yet there is only one leader. Just as it is with the people of God, we have only one head, one leader, Jesus Christ the "Lion of the tribe of Judah." (Revelation 5:5) When Jesus was here on this earth, he led groups of 3, 12, and 70. When building his core team, Jesus chose 12 men with absolutely no religious background to bring about the will of God, "on earth as it is in Heaven." (Matthew 6:10)

The point is this: Contrary to popular belief, building the most effective team is not about picking the most polished and educated team members. It is about picking the ones with the most potential, the ones who are the most committed to the cause, and the ones that aren't afraid to get their hands dirty! Entrepreneurs have the spirit of leadership.

Dominion

The hebrew word for dominion is "mamlakah," which means "royal power." Genesis 1:26 says, "Then God said, "Let us make man in our image, after our likeness. And let them have dominion over the fish of the sea and over the birds of the heavens and over the livestock and over all the earth and over every creeping thing that creeps on the earth." So, the essence of what the Lord is saying here is that we, as part of the government of Heaven, have been ordained by the King to dominate and control this earth as our domain. This is what an entrepreneur essentially does- take control! Not control of people, but of the earth, its systems and operations. For example, in practical terms, dominion looks like time management and goal setting.

In Habakkuk 2:2, God gives the man these instructions: "Write my answer plainly on tablets, so that a runner can carry the correct message to others." When dominion is being exercised, a vision is being made plain so that a multitude of people can catch it, benefit from it, and translate it to others within their sphere of influence.

Now, in Genesis 1:28, God says to Adam and Eve, "Fill the earth and subdue it." What does this mean? The Lord is commanding man to take control of the markets of the earth in ALL spheres. For example, can you imagine the amount of joy that would be created in the community if we as the people of God started buying and owning real estate that provided lower rental costs in a specific geography? The people who would benefit from this would truly be "the poor.." who Jesus said the Father had anointed him to bring the Good News to, before anyone else! (Luke 4:18) This would allow people to begin to save/invest more, do more for others, and have a better quality of life. In addition, what if we began to intentionally build relationships with these tenants and began to actively disciple them? The results would be enormous! We as the children of God have been called to control the markets of the earth, through the blessing of God, which we cover in Chapter 5.

The Entrepreneur, Accelerated Wealth Creator

There is a Jewish historical book called the Talmud that speaks of one's assets being 1/3 in land, 1/3 in business, and 1/3 kept liquid (Talmud (T. Bava Metzia 42a)) This is the ancient Hebrew formula for building wealth. Lets focus on the ☐ in business. Contrary to popular belief, most wealthy people's money is in their entity, their business, NOT in an investment account, and NOT in their personal home. When your focus is scaling the growth of a business, you do not have to wait in order to make money, like with an investment account, whether that is in the stock market or appreciation in a home. You are able to give, save, invest, make a profit, and grow the business all at the same time. The main point here is not to limit ourselves, but to expand our thinking to that of Genesis 1:28, "be fruitful and multiply." Isn't it interesting that God says to "multiply" and not simply to "add?" We must begin to shift our thinking into the realm of multiplication instead of just addition!

Poverty is a huge problem in our world today, even in America. The cause of most cases of poverty comes from a lack of self production. We can solve the problem of poverty by teaching people to live out Genesis 1:28, by becoming people that produce and increase! To be fruitful is to always be producing something, to multiply is to always be exponentially increasing. The easiest way to accomplish this is through becoming an entrepreneur and growing a company/companies.

The entrepreneur is also a master of FAITH. God is outside of time- so when we step out on faith, we bypass time, because faith is ALWAYS NOW (Hebrews 11:1)! Jesus turned water into wine. It usually takes a minimum of a month to pick the grapes and let them ferment, and that doesn't include the time it takes for the vines to grow! Jesus did it in five minutes.

John chapter 2:6-10 tells us: "Standing nearby were six stone water jars, used for Jewish ceremonial washing. Each could hold twenty to thirty gallons. Jesus told the servants, "Fill the jars with water." When the jars had been filled, he said, "Now dip some out, and take it to the master of ceremonies." So the servants followed his instructions.

When the master of ceremonies tasted the water that was now wine, not knowing where it had come from (though, of course, the servants knew), he called the bridegroom over. "A host always serves the best wine first," he said. "Then, when everyone has had a lot to drink, he brings out the less expensive wine. But you have kept the best until now!"

Jesus was an "Accelerated Wealth Creator."

Remember, an entrepreneur is a person of action. Take the political culture/climate that we have in America, where too many people settle for simply voting for a candidate that they think will change things and then waiting for the government to come and save them, or fix the problems in their city. Don't be that person. Vote if you want to, by all means, but don't leave it up to the government to right the ship, grab an oar yourself and start paddling!

Wallace Wattles, in his book, "The Science of Getting Rich," states:

"It is perfectly right that you give your best attention to the Science of Getting Rich, for it is the noblest and most necessary of all studies. If you neglect this study, you are derelict in your duty to yourself, to God and humanity; for you can render to God and humanity no greater service than to make the most of yourself."

Chapter 7
God's Economy, The Blessing

"That the blessing of Abraham might come on the Gentiles through Jesus Christ; that we might receive the promise of the Spirit through faith."
Galatians 3:14

God's Family- If God is IN you, THE BLESSING is on you!

"And now that you belong to Christ, you are the true children of Abraham. You are his heirs, and God's promise to Abraham belongs to you." (Galatians 3:29) God gave us Jesus as our spiritual blessing, but he also gave us the same natural blessing that He gave to Abraham.

Galatians 3:29 tells us that through Jesus Christ, God has blessed those who are in Christ with *the same* blessing that He blessed Abraham with! The same blessing that was on Adam in the garden was given to Abraham, and was fulfilled in Christ!

One variation of the hebrew word for "blessing" is "berakah" which literally means "an inheritance, or a tangible gift." This word, or some close variation of it, was used by God himself when He blessed Adam in the Garden and commissioned Abraham in the land of Haran.

This is the blessing that God gave to Abraham: "Now the Lord said to Abram (God later changed his name to "Abraham"), "Go from your country and your kindred and your father's house to the land that I will show you. And I will make you a great nation, and I will bless you and make your name great, so that you will be a blessing. I will bless those who bless you, and him who dishonors you I will curse, and in you all the families of the earth shall be blessed." Genesis 12:1-3. Genesis 13:2, some years later, tells us that Abram had become "very rich in livestock, silver, and gold." The livestock represent production- Abram's ability to make an income (his "business.") Silver represents exchange, the ability to interact with the world around him. Gold represents wealth accumulation, which shows us that Abram had amassed a very sizable fortune. This was the beginning of the fruit of the blessing that God bestowed upon Abram.

Deuteronomy 8:18 says, "You shall remember the Lord your God, for it is he who gives you power to get wealth, that he may confirm his covenant that he swore to your fathers, as it is this day." God is often referred to as "Father" in the scriptures. The term for father actually means "source." This passage is showing us that ALL WEALTH has its source in God. So, we would do well to never forget where the wealth comes from, and if we are ever in need, who to go to for help as well: God himself! Isaiah 55:8 says, "My thoughts are nothing like your thoughts," says the Lord. "And my ways are far beyond anything you could imagine." In other words, God's country and its laws/rules are completely different than anything we have ever known. It would do us a great deal of good to listen to the way God thinks and operates.

God's economy is 100% different from the economy we are used to living in. Here are just a few examples of how God's Kingdom economics function and how they are different form the ways of the natural world we live in today:

A few of God's Kingdom Principles found in His Constitution (The Bible):

A person's response to God's blessing determines the circumstances of his life. Most people are simply unaware or ignorant of what they possess in Christ! Phillipians 4:19 says, "And my God will supply every need of yours according to his riches in glory in Christ Jesus." You can imagine what type of wealth and riches God has, after all, he uses GOLD as asphalt and paves his streets with it! (Revelation 21:21)

The Big Ask: Jesus said, "Ask, and it will be given to you; seek, and you will find; knock, and it will be opened to you." Matthew 7:7.. Much of humanity's lack (of anything: finances, love, friends, health etc) today comes from simply not asking God.

Quite a few religious people will read this verse and put a different spin on it, but it is just what Jesus said. That's the problem with religion, it complicates things. God's Kingdom is not complicated, in fact, it is extremely simple. The only reason we struggle with living in its fullness is because it is drastically different from how we have already learned to live. Jesus also said, "If you ask me anything in my name, I will do it." John 14:14.. Again, don't overthink what he is saying here, just take it for what it is!

Kingdom Ambassadors: "So we are Christ's ambassadors; God is making his appeal through us." 2 Corinthians 5:20... Ambassadors are sent to be a representative of their home country. Ambassadors are taken care of by the country's government who sent them, and in that same way, when we come into the Kingdom of God we become "ambassadors for Christ." This means that the Kingdom of God supplies all of our needs! Philippians 4:19 says, "And this same God who takes care of me will supply all your needs from his glorious riches, which have been given to us in Christ Jesus."

The Principle of Kingdom Commonwealth: The principle of Commonwealth is a principle that most in our modern society are not familiar with at all. That is primarily because we do not practice this principle today. A commonwealth is a country that is founded for the common good of ALL people, in which every citizen has access to every resource. God's Kingdom is a commonwealth. It is founded on the principle found in 2 Peter 3:9, "...He does not want anyone to be destroyed..." The Lord's desire is that ALL men be saved, and this idea is found throughout God's Word multiple times. In a country that is a commonwealth, ALL people have access to ALL resources. 2 Peter 1:3 tells us that, "His divine power has granted to us ALL THINGS that pertain to life and godliness." Socialism attempts to manifest this idea, but without God as it's King. Any idea apart from God is doomed to fail, and that is why socialism is so dangerous, because it is so close to the real thing but is missing the most important piece: God as Lord and King. In God's Kingdom, everyone has access to all of His resources, but He is the King and He calls the shots, makes audibles, and establishes the rules. He is "judge, jury and executioner," as they say. God's Kingdom is a monarchy, where He has all power and authority. His Kingdom is a commonwealth, where ALL citizens have access to ALL resources.

Sowing and Reaping: "Don't be misled—you cannot mock the justice of God. You will always harvest what you plant." Galatians 6:7… This goes for everything in life, not just money!

"Honor the Lord with your wealth and with the best part of everything you produce. Then he will fill

your barns with grain, and your vats will overflow with good wine." Proverbs 3:9-10

"As long as the earth remains, there will be planting and harvest, cold and heat, summer and winter, day and night." Genesis 8:22

The world system focuses on buying and selling as it's primary economic principles, but the Kingdom focuses on sowing and reaping!

Giving to a King: When you give to a King he is automatically required to give you more than you gave. This is a direct reflection of his own wealth and reputation. You can't outgive the King of Kings- because he owns everything! So, if you want to be prosperous, give to the King who owns it all! Tithing is also a very important principle in the Kingdom. The tithe is the connector to the physical blessing of the Lord. Debt is the umbilical cord of the world's system, tithing is the umbilical cord to the Kingdom. The tithe is defined as ten percent of all increase, or income. Think of the tithe as a holy tax, that is set up by the King. God only asks for 10% of our income, and lets us keep 90%! After all, he owns all of it anyways. He only asks for 10% in return to show our trust in Him. Now, you're not going to go to Hell if you dont give 10% of your income to the work of the Kingdom, but God's Word is clear, the devourer will not be rebuked for you. Malachi 3:10,11 says, "Bring the full tithe into the storehouse, so that there may be food in My

The Way of Wealth

house. Test Me in this," says the LORD of Hosts. "See if I will not open the windows of heaven and pour out for you blessing without measure. I will rebuke the devourer for you, so that it will not destroy the fruits of your land, and the vine in your field will not fail to produce fruit," says the LORD of Hosts."

This "holy tax" is designed to show God that He can trust us, especially in the area of money. It is to show God that we trust Him to take care of us more than we trust our money to take care of us. In the same way that we are protected by our American government because of our citizenship and the taxes we pay, it is the same with the Kingdom of Heaven. Taxes usually have a negative connotation, but in God's Kingdom, taxes are solely for our benefit and completely free from corruption!

Faith: Faith is the currency of God's Kingdom. Currency is defined simply as a medium of exchange. All that God requires of us in order to receive in His Kingdom is the FAITH that it can happen! Luke 8:43-48 tells us the story of a woman who used the faith that she had in order to be healed: "A woman in the crowd had suffered for twelve years with constant bleeding, and she could find no cure. Coming up behind Jesus, she touched the fringe of his robe. Immediately, the bleeding stopped.

"Who touched me?" Jesus asked.

Everyone denied it, and Peter said, "Master, this whole crowd is pressing up against you."

But Jesus said, "Someone deliberately touched me, for I felt healing power go out from me." When the woman realized that she could not stay hidden, she began to tremble and fell to her knees in front of him. The whole crowd heard her explain why she had touched him and that she had been immediately healed. "Daughter," he said to her, "your faith has made you well. Go in peace."

This woman BELIEVED that Jesus not only COULD heal her, but WOULD!

If you are not a member of God's family and a citizen of His country, I encourage you to take action right now. You can commit your life to Him right where you sit today. Romans 10:9-10 says, "If you openly declare that Jesus is Lord and believe in your heart that God raised him from the dead, you will be saved. For it is by believing in your heart that you are made right with God, and it is by openly declaring your faith that you are saved."

This isn't about making money, coming to God so that you can be blessed (although that will happen, if that's your reason for trying to start a relationship with Him, I warn you, God will not be mocked), joining a church or becoming "religious." This is about beginning a personal, individual relationship with the Creator of the universe, who just

The Way of Wealth

so happens to be your Father. Trust me, I can tell you from personal experience, He is the best dad ever, and I have a pretty great earthly father!

CHAPTER 8
PHILANTHROPY & GIVING

"Though one may be overpowered, two can defend themselves." Ecclesiastes 4:12

"If you want to go fast, go alone, if you want to go far, go together!" -African Proverb

TOGETHER

Chit Fund: The power of "together"

A Chit fund is where a group of people agree to periodically pool a certain amount of money together in the same fund- to which every member has access to in the future. It is used as both a savings tool and a credit tool. It provides the group who put into it the flexibility to leverage larger amounts of capital, while only contributing a smaller amount. This idea originated in Indian culture as a means to advance the entire group

The Way of Wealth

or family financially. For example, if there are 10 people in a group who each contribute $250 per month for 1 year, they will have $30,000 in the fund at the end of year 1. So now, the group has a plethora of ways it can handle this $30,000. They can place a down payment on a home for one of its members, purchase a small business that increases the income for every member, or simply place it in an account that gets 5%-10% and let it grow for several years and then distribute the money how they would like.

This is just a small glimpse into the idea of teamwork that God had in mind when he began the church! Now let's examine what would happen if we came together and followed God's plan for his people.

"No Plan B!"

God's plan to end poverty and hunger: the EKKLESIA. Ekklesia is the Greek word that Jesus used to describe "church." Over the years, especially in the West, we have deviated from Jesus' definition of what the church should be. The Ekklesia as Jesus described it is defined as "a political assembly of citizens." I would put it like this: an assembly of the citizens of Heaven, here on earth, whose primary mission is to bring their country, Heaven, to the earth. The church is a group of people in direct vertical relationship with God resulting in a horizontal relationship with others. Now that we have redefined the word "church," we can see how the church is God's plan for bringing change to the world. The church should be the most influential entity on the face of the earth. If we gave "together" as the church, what could we accomplish?

Example:

There are 240 million people in America who identify as "Christian." Lets just say the average income of an American individual is $42,000 a year. The tithe on that would be $4,200. If every Christian individual tithed 10% of their income at $4,200 every year the total amount would be: $1,008,000,000,000! That's over $1 trillion! Just imagine what we could do with that amount of giving, EVERY YEAR!

— The National debt could be wiped out in 25-35 years.

— Every single missionary could be fully funded- both foreign and domestic.

— We could completely eliminate world hunger, starvation, and deaths from preventable diseases.

— Illiteracy could vanish.

— All water and sanitation problems could be solved.

— What else?

All of this could happen WITHIN OUR OWN LIFE TIMES! This is the vision of the "EKKLESIA" church that God has- and has had since the beginning. This is the true potential and PLAN for the church, but we can only accomplish this if we GIVE TOGETHER! We have to shift our thinking from "ME" to "WE!" Did you know that two horses can actually pull FOUR times the amount of weight that one horse could pull by itself? That's the power of "TOGETHER."

Giving is not just about helping others- which it most certainly is first and foremost. Giving creates the space in YOUR life for God to increase YOU. We are not talking about being greedy here, we are talking about GROWING our capacity to receive from God so that we can give more than we did before.

"A man reaps what he sows." Galatians 6:7

It's time to go from "making a living" to "making a GIVING!"

Four Types of Giving in the Bible

The Bible is God's constitution for his country. It has knowledge and insight for us on how to practically live in the realm of finance.

Philanthropy & Giving

Let's take a look at the four types of giving that the Bible speaks about:

1. **First Fruits:**
   "Honor the Lord with your wealth, and with the firstfruits of all your produce; then your barns will be filled with plenty, and your vats will be bursting with wine." Proverbs 3:9,10
   a. Giving first fruits to God shows that a person is generous, gracious, and shows God that they are not in love with money! The firstfruits show God that He can trust you with money.
   b. It is off the top of your income- before you do anything else with it.
   c. All in all, there are 31 references in the Bible that concern the firstfruits.

2. **Tithe:**
   Matthew 23:23, Jesus said you should. While tithing is not his main point here in this passage, he still says that you should do it. If Jesus says it, that settles it. Jesus is our Lord and King, what he says, goes.
   a. Tithing shows an individual's obedience and faithfulness
   b. Tithing is the divine connector to the overflowing blessing (Malachi 3:10)
   c. Tithing is the way for recession and depression to bypass you, "I will rebuke the devourer for your sake." (Malachi 3:11)

d. 10% of ALL income. (Increase)
e. Rate of Return= Protection from loss.
3. **Alms or Charity** to the poor:
Proverbs 19:17 says, "Whoever is generous to the poor lends to the Lord, he will repay him for his deed."
   a. Alms/Charity comes out of compassion for the poor and those in need.
   b. Alms/Charity should be given in secret to protect the dignity of the one in distress. Matthew 6:3,4 says, "But when you give to someone in need, don't let your left hand know what your right hand is doing. Give your gifts in private, and your Father, who sees everything, will reward you."
   c. Rate of Return = reimbursement
4. **Seed**:
Matthew 13:8 says, "Still other seeds fell on fertile soil, and they produced a crop that was thirty, sixty, and even a hundred times as much as had been planted!"
   a. Seed giving is motivated by FAITH in God and the REWARD of God.
   b. The seed is the surest way to stop poverty in your life.
   c. Seed giving is the quickest way for total debt cancellation.
   d. The seed must be in fertile soil in order for it to accomplish the impossible in life. Jesus used farming analogies

to show us how the Kingdom of God works.

e. Rate of Return= 30, 60, and 100 fold.

A lot of people have tried to live by just one or two of these principles and then begin to wonder why they don't become prosperous. The main reason for this is because they have turned one type of giving into another- and these are spiritual LAWS, you can not violate them and expect a different result. Each type of giving has its own rate of return. Let's say Wall Street pays 10% for a fund, and 5% for another… it would be foolish of me to take my money from the 10% fund, put it in the 5% fund and still expect to receive 10%. The point here is this: Don't change your tithe into alms, seed into tithe, or alms into seed. God won't rebuke the devourer if you change the rate of return on your own by changing where you put your money.

God has given us a game plan for our financial lives- we need only to read His Word and follow it. Hosea 4:6 says, "My people are destroyed for lack of knowledge." I pray that you take the knowledge of His word and apply it to your finances. If you do, get ready for an avalanche of blessing to overtake you! (Deuteronomy 28:2)

CHAPTER 9
GET ON YOUR WAY OF WEALTH

"I pray that you may prosper even as your soul prospers." - 3 John 1:2

If you want to make an impact on society and provide freedom for you and your family, then you have to act now. Even if you made $1,000,000 a year, it would still take 1,000 years to become a billionaire! *"today is the day of salvation." (2 Corinthians 6:1). We are not saying that money and salvation are synonymous, but rather that you must take action now with your finances if you want to achieve financial freedom.*

How do we create this for YOU and your family:

1. Why are you doing this? For who, what, why?
2. Write your numbers down
   a. Income/Expenses
   b. Assets/Liabilities

    c. Schedule appointment with Golden Gryphon Private Wealth
3. Focus on Cash Flow
    a. Cash is not king; CASH FLOW is King. Income–expenses = Cash flow
    b. Cashflow provides flexibility and freedom
    c. How much income do you have left after expenses?
4. Identify weak spots in your finances
    a. You can't shrink your way to wealth, but what can you cut out for the time being?
    b. 9/10 people spend too much on eating out
    c. What is your net worth? Assets–Liabilities =Net Worth
5. Take action
    a. Set up a family banking policy
    b. Buy precious metals
    c. Decrease expenses
    d. Start a business
    e. Acquire rental properties
    f. Track your progress and multiply again and again
    g. Invest into yourself

www.ingramcontent.com/pod-product-compliance
Lightning Source LLC
Chambersburg PA
CBHW070501220526
45466CB00004B/1911